THE CHILDREN'S GUIDE TO ASTRAL PROJECTION

J. A. HOMES

BRASS
TACKS
PRESS

LOS ANGELES

2015

BRASS TACKS PRESS
WEBSITE: www.brasstackspress.com
EMAIL: brasstackspress@yahoo.com

© December 2003 by Brass Tacks Press
2nd Edition © July 2015

LIBRARY OF CONGRESS IN PUBLICATION DATA
J. A. Homes
The Children's Guide to Astral Projection
ISBN: 978-0-9820140-2-8
Printed in the USA

FOREWORD

Awareness of the Astral - World is a gift. Not unlike musical ability, athletic talent, or a powerful mind, it can be developed and explored, or ignored and neglected. While it slowly fades into the background of our busy lives.

Still, it is always there, and occasionally it will appear spontaneously, thrusting itself into our familiar world, much to our surprise.

For those not prepared, or at least willing to accept the occasional overlapping of these different worlds, you can expect some anxiety, or even a cycle of fear, as you struggle to find an explanation that will push away these often, un-explainable experiences.

With this volume, it is both, the gifted and the confused that I wish to serve.

I make no apologies for the complex ideas that are presented here. There is nothing here that is not litterally built into your physical body.

The astral plane is the natural domain of children, poets, and young creatives. They know this world, and you know they know.

LOVE AND GREAT
RESPECT.

J.A. Homes

fOR

Daisy

EVERYTHING IS VIBRATING.
= MAKE A FART NOISE,
DO IT NOW.

PFFFLP

PFFFLLL PRPPLT!!
THAT IS THE SOUND
of your MOUTH VIBRATING.

LIGHT

LIGHT IS TINY STRINGS of ENERGY
...VIBRATING

MATTER, THE VERY STUFF OF...

YOUR BODY

HEAD → NECK → HAND → WIENER → FARM → LEG

THE EARTH

A CHAIR

A ROCK,

SPACE

A CAT

ALL IS MADE OUT OF TINY PIECES OF ENERGY,

Vibrating

MUSIC, SUCH AS THE SOUND OF A VIOLIN, IS THE SOUND OF THE VIBRATION OF THE STRINGS.

SUN-LIGHT MAKES A SOUND, BUT WE CANNOT HEAR IT.

SUN IS SO POWERFUL AND SO HIGH, THAT IT IS BEYOND OUR ABILITY TO HEAR.

THE EARTH WE LIVE ON, MAKES A SOUND ALSO, SO DEEP AND LOW...

THAT MOST OF US CANNOT HEAR IT AT ALL.

WHAT WE SEE HEAR TOUCH THINK

IS VIBRATION

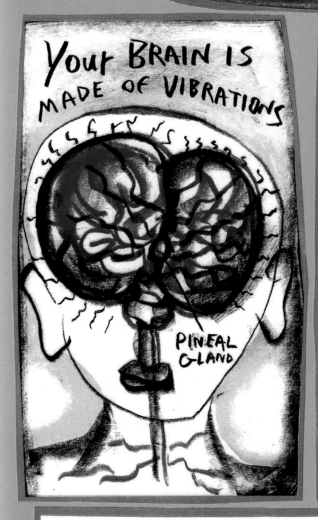

Your BRAIN IS MADE OF VIBRATIONS

PINEAL GLAND

YOUR THOUGHTS TOO,

ARE VIBRATIONS.

JUST LIKE THE SUNLIGHT, YOUR THOUGHTS ARE TINY STRINGS OF ENERGY, WIGGLING ALL AROUND.

4

MEMORY

DO YOU REMEMBER THE FIRST HOUSE THAT YOU EVER LIVED IN? OR...

YOUR GRANDMA'S VOICE?

THE WAY TO SCHOOL?

BREAKFAST?

MEMORY, IS A VERY SPECIAL KIND OF VIBRATION.

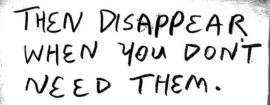

THEN DISAPPEAR WHEN YOU DON'T NEED THEM.

THAT IS, THEY MOVE OUT OF YOUR RANGE OF PERCEPTION.

WHERE DO THEY GO?

DREAMS ARE LIKE THIS ALSO.

WE CAN BE HAVING ALL KINDS OF RADICAL ADVENTURES—

THESE EXPERIENCES HAVE JUST MOVED UP TO THE NEXT VIBRATIONAL LEVEL, OR RATHER YOUR MIND HAS RETURNED TO THE MATERIAL LEVEL. WHAT WE USUALLY SEE, FEEL, AND HEAR.

WHERE IS THE ASTRAL PLANE? JUST LIKE YOUR MEMORIES ARE STILL THERE, EVEN WHEN YOU AREN'T THINKING THEM, OR THE SUN IS SHINING EVEN WHEN IT IS NIGHTTIME, THE ASTRAL PLANE...

-IS RIGHT HERE, RIGHT NOW, EVEN AS YOU READ THIS BOOK.

THINGS ARE HAPPENING ALL AROUND YOU ALL THE TIME ON THE ASTRAL LEVEL. PEOPLE ARE CHECKING YOU OUT, THINGS ARE FLYING BY.

EVEN NOW, YOU ARE DOING THINGS, ON AN ASTRAL LEVEL. EVEN IF YOU HARDLY NOTICE IT.

A PART OF YOU.

ALWAYS NOTICES.

THE FIRST THING YOU NEED TO DO, TO BECOME AWARE OF THE ASTRAL WORLD, IS SIMPLY TO GIVE IT YOUR ATTENTION.

ATTENTION IS A REAL SUBSTANCE. LIKE AIR OR LIGHT, IT CANNOT BE TOUCHED. IN THE MATERIAL WORLD, IT IS SOMETHING WE WANT FROM OUR FRIENDS AND FAMILY. WE HAVE ALL FELT HOW PAINFUL IT IS TO FEEL LONELY OR BE IGNORED.

IN NEED OF ATTENTION.

ON THE ASTRAL LEVEL, ATTENTION ACTS AS A POWERFUL LINE OF ENERGY THAT BEAMS OUT OF EVERY LIVING THING.

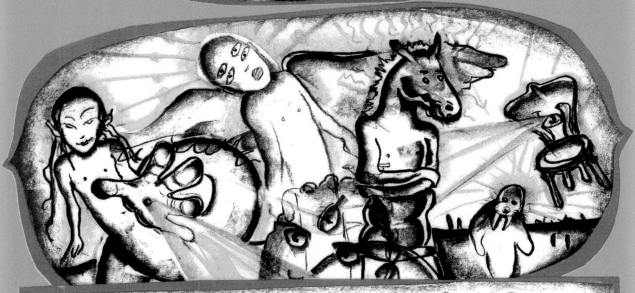

ATTENTION IS THE MEASURE OF LIFE AND POWER, IN THE MATERIAL WORLD AS WELL AS THE ASTRAL. POWERFUL BEINGS HAVE A LOT OF ATTENTION.

THE POWER OF ATTENTION, IS THE LINK BETWEEN THE ASTRAL AND MATERIAL WORLDS. THIS IS YOUR BRIDGE.

EVEN HERE IN THE MATERIAL WORLD, ATTENTION IS VITAL. A BABY, IF NOT GIVEN LOTS OF LIFE-GIVING ATTENTION...

IS ALMOST CERTAIN TO FADE AWAY AND DIE. NO DOUBT ABOUT IT. LOVE IS THE MOST POWERFUL FORM OF ATTENTION

YOUR HUMAN BODY IS MADE MOSTLY OF WATER, SALTS AND MINERALS. YOUR WHOLE BODY TOGETHER IS A BIG BATTERY. IT STORES UP THE LIGHT-ENERGY CALLED "ATTENTION."

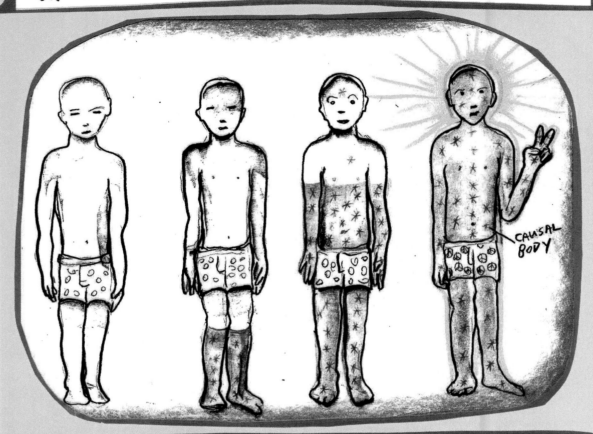

THIS BATTERY FUNCTION IS KNOWN AS THE "CAUSAL BODY." A LITTLE BABY NEEDS HER CAUSAL BODY CHARGED UP ALL THE TIME UNTIL SHE IS STRONG ENOUGH TO GIVE AND RECEIVE ATTENTION CONSCIOUSLY ON HER OWN.

SOME KIDS SEEM UNABLE TO HOLD THEIR ATTENTION. THEY JUMP FROM ONE THING TO ANOTHER, SOMETIMES DISPLAYING ANNOYING "ATTENTION GETTING" BEHAVIOR.

SOME DOCTORS CALL THIS "A.D.D." (ATTENTION DEFICIT DISORDER). THEY GIVE THESE KIDS VERY STRONG MEDICINE TO MAKE THEM CONCENTRATE. HOWEVER, THESE KIDS ARE ACTUALLY SUFFERING FROM A KIND OF STARVATION OF THEIR CAUSAL BODIES. THEY NEED YOUR HELP AND UNDERSTANDING.

LOVE, PATIENCE, ATTENTION AND ATTENTION-BUILDING EXERCISES COULD CURE THIS SAD CONDITION EASILY.

PROTECTION

IT IS IMPORTANT BEFORE MAKING THE JUMP INTO ANOTHER WORLD — KNOW HOW TO ASK FOR PROTECTION.

— AT FIRST,

YOU MAY FIND THIS BRAVE NEW WORLD FOGGY, CONFUSING, EVEN SCARY. HOWEVER YOU ARE NOT ALONE, YOU HAVE FRIENDS.

BRIGHT BEINGS ARE, EVEN NOW, HANGING AROUND, KEEPING AN EYE ON YOU AND YOUR PROGRESS. MAKING SURE YOU'RE O.K.

SOME CALL THESE TEACHERS "ANGELS" THEY HAVE BEEN WITH YOU SINCE BEFORE YOU WERE BORN, WATCHING, GUIDING YOU.

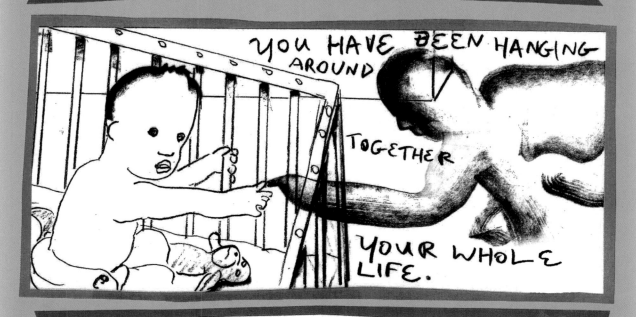

VERY OFTEN, YOU MEET IN DREAMS, ONLY TO FORGET THEM WHEN YOU WAKE.

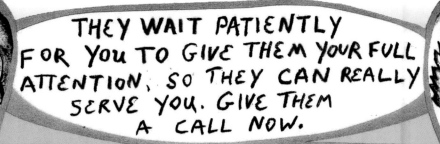

THEY WAIT PATIENTLY FOR YOU TO GIVE THEM YOUR FULL ATTENTION, SO THEY CAN REALLY SERVE YOU. GIVE THEM A CALL NOW.

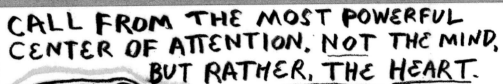

FIND A SAFE, QUIET, COMFORTABLE PLACE TO BE. YOUR BED, OR FAVORITE CHAIR FOR INSTANCE. GET A BLANKET, RELAX, TAKE A FEW DEEP BREATHS. NOW CALL TO THEM.

CALL FROM THE MOST POWERFUL CENTER OF ATTENTION, NOT THE MIND, BUT RATHER, THE HEART.

THIS IS WEIRD, BUT HERE GOES! HEY ANGEL! Yoo Hoo! I NEED SOME HELP HERE! CAN YOU DO THAT FOR ME?

SO, IT BEGINS

YOUR BREATHING BECOMES VERY IMPORTANT AT THIS POINT. Comfortable??? GOOD!

FROM NOW ON YOU WILL BE AWARE OF YOUR BREATHING. ARE YOU BREATHING DEEP? OR SHALLOW? ARE YOU BREATHING FAST? OR SLOW? BREATH IS YOUR CONTROL UNIT, AND LINK TO THE BODY.

THEN, IF ANYTHING COMES UP, THAT IS WEIRD OR UPSETTING, YOU CAN CHECK YOUR BREATHING! DEEP EVEN BREATHING IS BEST!

ARE YOU READY?

YOU'll BE FINE!

THERE ARE MANY WAYS TO GET IN CONTACT WITH THE ASTRAL PLANE. IT IS IMPORTANT HERE THAT WE KEEP TO THE BASICS. SO WE WILL START WITH A SIMPLE TECHNIQUE, THIS ONE WAS GIVEN TO ME BY MY FRIEND CHRISTINE. IT IS SIMPLE, AND CAN BE VERY EFFECTIVE. BUT DON'T THINK THAT IF IT'S "SIMPLE", IT'S EASY.

FIRST, GET COMFORTABLE. BREATHE. FEEL ALL THE SKIN ON YOUR BODY, FROM THE INSIDE. TAKE YOUR TIME. NOW, WITH EACH BREATH, COUNT BACKWARDS FROM 100... 99... 98... 97... AND SO ON, TO ZERO. BREATHE EACH NUMBER.

19

AT FIRST YOU WILL SEE NOTHING ~

SOON YOU MAY SEE COLORS ~ AND SENSE MOVEMENT.

YOU MIGHT EVEN SENSE A STRANGE "FLOATING" FEELING...

...KEEP COUNTING

3-2-1-ZERO

YOU ARE AT ZERO, BREATHING DEEP AND EVENLY. WAIT. A BEING STANDS BEFORE YOU. THERE MIGHT BE MANY PEOPLE, CURIOUSLY CROWDED AROUND. ONE SPECIAL PERSON STANDS WAITING.

HE OR SHE WILL BE ABSOLUTELY FAMILIAR — TO YOU.

YOU KNOW EACH OTHER VERY WELL.

THIS IS YOUR GUARDIAN — HE OR SHE IS HERE TO HELP YOU NOW.

THE LIGHT OF ATTENTION

AT THIS MOMENT YOU MUST GIVE YOUR FULL ATTENTION TO THIS ONE PERSON. THIS IS YOUR FIRST BIG TEST ON THE ASTRAL PLANE, AND IT MAY AFFECT YOUR WHOLE JOURNEY. SO FOCUS AND HOLD ATTENTION.

IF YOU CAN GIVE THIS BEING YOUR FULLEST ATTENTION, HE WILL "LIGHT UP." OBSERVE THE EYES, FACE, FORM, ATTITUDE...

BREATHE - TAKE IN WHAT YOU SEE...

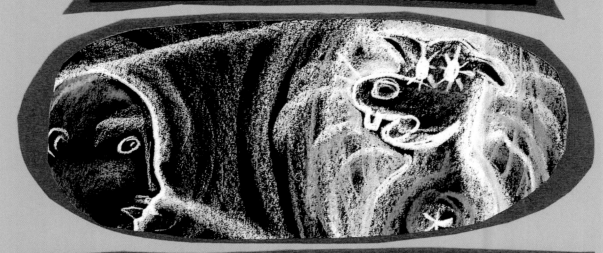

IT CAN BE PRETTY WEIRD AT FIRST...

UNDERSTAND THAT NO MATTER HOW THIS
RE-CONNECTION WITH YOUR GUARDIAN
HAPPENS, IT IS A GOOD THING. WHEN IT
HAPPENED TO ME, I FREAKED OUT COMPLETELY
AND SHOT BACK INTO MY BODY. IT WAS STILL
A VALUABLE EXPERIENCE, HOWEVER WEIRD.

VERY OFTEN THIS FIRST MEETING CAN BE A
SHOCKING EXPERIENCE. BE PREPARED.

IF YOU ARE FREAKING OUT, NOT BREATHING
PROPERLY, YOUR ATTENTION MAY GET DISTORTED
BY YOUR CONTRACTING EMOTIONAL CENTER.
(MORE ON THIS LATER)-THIS CAN CAUSE THINGS TO
APPEAR TWISTED AND SCARY, THUS FREAKING
YOU OUT MORE-ETC. FORTUNATELY THIS IS AN
EASY PROBLEM TO SOLVE. TAKE A DEEP BREATH.

BACK ON THE ASTRAL PLANE: SO YOU'RE STANDING BEFORE THIS BEING THAT YOU HAVE KNOWN FOREVER BUT YOU DON'T KNOW HIS/HER NAME! PUT YOUR ATTENTION ON YOUR HEART CENTER...

MAKE THIS REQUEST THROUGH YOUR HEART...

PLEASE, TELL ME YOUR NAME.

NOW SOMETHING AMAZING SHOULD HAPPEN... I CANNOT SAY EXACTLY WHAT, AS IT IS SO DIFFERENT FOR EACH PERSON. SOMETHING LIKE A STREAM OF IMAGES, FORGOTTEN MEMORIES, DREAMY INFORMATION WILL COME POURING OUT OF THIS BEING, INTO YOUR HEART THEN UP INTO YOUR MIND...

DID YOU CATCH THE NAME?

IF YOU DID GET A NAME, YOU'RE LUCKY. REPEAT IT AND COMMIT IT TO MEMORY. THIS NAME WILL HELP YOU TO REMEMBER THINGS, LOST OBJECTS, LIVES YOU LIVED AND OTHER COOL STUFF. IF NOT, AT LEAST YOU MADE CONTACT.

AFTER THIS, ANYTHING COULD HAPPEN→

YOU MIGHT: VISIT PEOPLE AT HOME!

MEET WEIRDOS.

TRAVEL AIMLESSLY

ANYTHING AND EVERYTHING CAN AND WILL HAPPEN. WHAT YOU DO IS LIMITED ONLY BY THE STRENGTH IN YOUR CAUSAL BODY. WHICH, BY THE WAY, IS VERY TOUGH AND WILL LAST YOU QUITE A LOT LONGER THAN YOUR MATERIAL BODY.

BEFORE WE GO ANY FURTHER, I WOULD LIKE TO MENTION THE VITAL IMPORTANCE OF MAKING A RECORD OF YOUR TRAVELS AND EXPERIENCES. MEMORIES OF THE ASTRAL WORLD HAVE A VERY STRANGE QUALITY ———→

SIMILAR TO DREAMS. AS DESCRIBED BEFORE, THE ASTRAL WORLD IS VIBRATING A BIT FASTER THAN THE MATERIAL WORLD. SO, LESSONS AS WELL AS EXPERIENCES, CLEARLY SEEN...

CAN SLIP AWAY COMPLETELY. OFTEN THE COMPLEX, FADING VISIONS ARE IMPOSSIBLE TO FIND AGAIN. SO DO YOURSELF A FAVOR, GET A PAD OF PAPER, AND WRITE, DRAW AND REMEMBER YOUR EXPERIENCES and FEELINGS.

IT IS CLEAR THAT NON-TRAVELERS CAN OFTEN HAVE A VERY HARD TIME UNDERSTANDING THE CURIOUS WORLD OF THE ASTRAL-TRAVELERS. SOMETIMES PEOPLE VERY CLOSE TO US CAN FREAK OUT, THINKING WE HAVE BECOME SICK OR CRAZY OR WORSE. IT IS EASY TO AVOID THIS PROBLEM. BE SMART, AND ONLY SHARE YOUR NOTES AND DISCOVERIES WITH THE PEOPLE THAT REALLY TRUST AND UNDERSTAND YOU.

27

ON EARTH, AS IT IS ON THE ASTRAL PLANE, THERE IS ALWAYS MORE TO DISCOVER, MORE LESSONS, EVER DEEPER LAYERS OF EXPERIENCE.

IF YOU HAVE HAD ANY SUCCESS AT ALL AT BREAKING OUT OF THE MATERIAL WORLD YOU HAVE FOUND THAT YOU HAVE A VERY LIMITED SUPPLY OF POWER, IN THE FORM OF ATTENTION. IN THE ASTRAL WORLD "ATTENTION" IS KNOWN AS "LIGHT" AND IS THE ONLY FORM OF POWER OR ENERGY. IN FACT THE WHOLE PLACE IS MADE OUT OF LIGHT, NOT UNLIKE THIS WORLD.

SO, HOW DO YOU GET MORE OF THIS FORM OF POWER? WELL, WHAT DO YOU DO IF YOU WANT TO BUILD YOURSELF BIG STRONG MUSCLES?...

TO BUILD UP ATTENTION IN YOUR CAUSAL BODY, HERE IS ONE SIMPLE EXERCISE YOU CAN DO IN BED, BEFORE GOING TO SLEEP AT NIGHT.

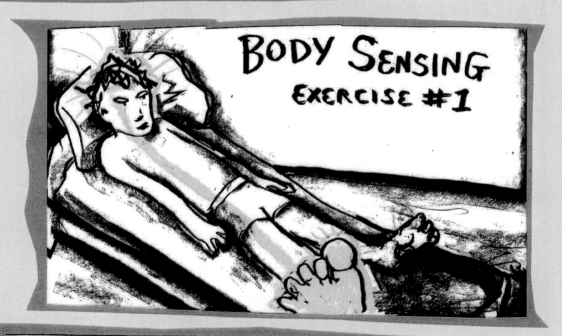

FIRST, GET COMFORTABLE, DON'T FORGET YOUR BREATH. BREATHE DEEP + EVENLY.

PAY ATTENTION! ① TO YOUR RIGHT FOOT. DON'T LOOK AT IT! DON'T IMAGINE IT! SENSE IT, FEEL IT FROM INSIDE.

② AS SOON AS YOUR RIGHT FOOT FEELS AS IF IT IS DISSAPPEARING, SWITCH, AND SENSE YOUR LEFT FOOT.

③ NOW GO TO YOUR RIGHT ANKLE. SENSE THE LEG RIGHT UP TO THE KNEE.

④ NOW SENSE YOUR LEFT LEG.

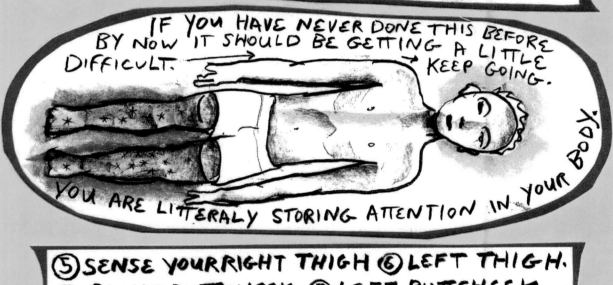

IF YOU HAVE NEVER DONE THIS BEFORE BY NOW IT SHOULD BE GETTING A LITTLE DIFFICULT. KEEP GOING.

YOU ARE LITTERALY STORING ATTENTION IN YOUR BODY.

⑤ SENSE YOUR RIGHT THIGH ⑥ LEFT THIGH.
⑦ RIGHT BUTTCHEEK. ⑧ LEFT BUTTCHEEK.
⑨ SENSE YOUR GUTS, BUNGHOLE, GENITALIA.
⑩ STOMACH MUSCLES, BELLYBUTTON ⑪ LOW BACK.
⑫ CHEST, LUNGS, HEART. ⑬ UPPER BACK.
⑭ RIGHT HAND. ⑮ LEFT HAND.
⑯ RIGHT FOREARM ⑰ LEFT FOREARM.
⑱ RIGHT BICEP. ⑲ LEFT BICEP.

YOUR BODY IS A BIG BATTERY. CHARGED WITH LIGHT.

20) SOLAR PLEXUS, THROAT. 21) BACK OF NECK, SPINE. 22) BACK OF THE SKULL. 23) JAW AND MOUTH. 24) FACE, FRONT OF SKULL. 25) SENSE THE INSIDE OF YOUR HEAD - NOW BREATHE, TEN BREATHS.

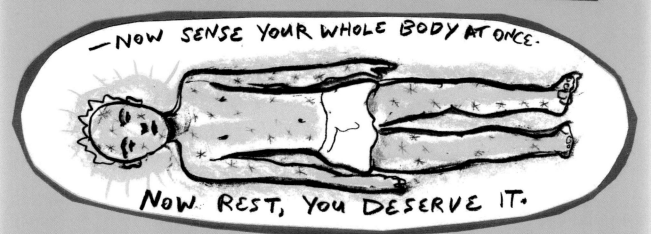

—NOW SENSE YOUR WHOLE BODY AT ONCE.

NOW REST, YOU DESERVE IT.

BREATHING THROUGH THE TOP OF YOUR HEAD.

EXERCISE #2

HERE IS ANOTHER EXERCISE TO BUILD UP LIGHT IN YOUR CAUSAL BODY. AT FIRST, YOU MUST BE ASKING, "WHAT COULD I POSSIBLY BREATHE THROUGH THE ROOF OF MY SKULL?" WELL, REMEMBER WHEN I TOLD YOU THAT THE WORLD IS MADE OF ENERGY VIBRATING? THAT ENERGY, IN ITS RAW FORM, IS FLOWING AROUND YOU AND THE WORLD AND EVERY-THING, ALL THE TIME. IN THE EASTERN WORLD WE CALL THIS LIVING ENERGY "PRANA".

WHAT IS... PRANA?

LOOK UP IN THE SKY ON A CLEAR DAY. NOTICE THE LITTLE SPARKLING PARTICLES OF ENERGY AS THEY SWIRL AROUND. THIS IS PRANA. YOU CAN BREATHE THIS STUFF DOWN THROUGH THE TOP OF YOUR HEAD AND COLLECT IT INTO A SPINNING BALL OF LIGHT IN THE CENTER OF YOUR BELLY. HERE'S HOW...

SIT COMFORTABLY, INHALE, SENSE THE PRANA FLOWING THROUGH THE TOP OF YOUR HEAD, INTO YOUR BELLY.

EXHALE, USE YOUR ATTENTION TO FORM A BALL OF ENERGY ABOUT THE SIZE OF YOUR HEAD.

REPEAT...

CONTINUE TO DO THIS FOR AS LONG AS YOU CAN, UNTIL YOUR WHOLE BODY IS FILLED WITH LIGHT. SENSE YOUR FOOT, IS IT PULSING? ON YOUR LAST BREATH BEFORE STOPPING, MAKE THE BALL OF LIGHT SPIN AS FAST AS YOU CAN. THEN, AS YOU EXHALE LET THE SPINNING BALL OF LIGHT EXPAND. MAKE IT →

SURROUND YOUR BODY.

EXHALE.

IF YOU DO THESE KINDS OF ATTENTION-BUILDING EXERCISES, IT WILL NOT BE LONG BEFORE YOUR CAUSAL BODY IS PRETTY MUCH CHARGED UP ALL THE TIME. THIS MEANS YOU WILL BE IN WHAT IS KNOWN AS AN "EXPANDED STATE."

EXPANSION and CONTRACTION

THE FLOW OF YOUR ATTENTION IS ALWAYS DOING ONE OF TWO THINGS. EITHER <u>EXPANDING</u> OUTWARD, OR IT IS <u>CONTRACTING</u> INWARD. OFTEN WE DO NOT EVEN NOTICE THIS AUTOMATIC REFLEX. WE DO, HOWEVER, NOTICE HOW IT MAKES OUR BODIES FEEL.

CALM, —
LOOSE, — OPEN.
FREE, —
LIGHT, —

THIS IS
EXPANSION...

AGITATED, —
TIGHT, — CLOSED.
CONSTRICTED. —
HEAVY, —

THIS IS HOW
CONTRACTION FEELS.

KNOW THIS - YOUR ATTENTION IS EXPANDING AND CONTRACTING ALL THE TIME WITHOUT YOUR KNOWLEDGE. IF YOU "LIKE" SOMETHING OR SOMEONE, YOU EXPAND TOWARDS THEM. IF YOU "DON'T LIKE", YOU CONTRACT AWAY FROM THEM. SIMPLE, HAPPY-EXPAND AFRAID → CONTRACT. IN-OUT, IN-OUT, YOUR WHOLE LIFE LONG.

SENSE YOUR BODY NOW... ARE YOU EXPANDING OR ARE YOU CONTRACTING? — CONGRATULATIONS! YOU ARE PAYING ATTENTION TO YOUR ATTENTION! THIS IS A GREAT MOMENT FOR YOU!

34

NOW THAT YOU CAN PAY ATTENTION TO YOUR ATTENTION, YOU HAVE TAKEN A FIRST STEP TO BEING ABLE TO CONTROL YOUR EXPANSIONS AND CONTRACTIONS OF THE ENERGY-BODY ON THE ASTRAL PLANE!

LET'S SAY YOU ARE OUT FLYING AROUND, AND YOU MAKE CONTACT WITH A STRANGE BEING.

FOR SOME REASON YOU GET SCARED, YOUR ATTENTION-LIGHT STARTS TO CONTRACT. THINGS START LOOKING WEIRD!

THIS JUST MAKES YOU MORE SCARED, SO YOU CONTRACT HARDER. THINGS JUST GET WEIRDER.

WHAT DO YOU DO?

PAY ATTENTION TO YOUR ATTENTION!

AND DON'T FORGET TO CALL YOUR GUARDIANS FOR SUPPORT

SENSE YOUR FOOT. WHAT IS YOUR STATE? ARE YOU CONTRACTING OR EXPANDING? IS YOUR ATTENTION SQUIRMING AND FREAKING OUT, TRYING TO ESCAPE? GOOD! GO WITH IT, NEVER TRY TO RESIST A CONTRACTION. THE ONLY WAY OUT IS THROUGH.

SURRENDER TO IT COMPLETELY.

BREATHE BREATHE! THEN...

BOUNCE! BACK INTO AN ➝

EXPANDED STATE.

THE ONLY OTHER WAY TO DEAL WITH A CONTRACTION LIKE THIS ONE IS TO "DROP OUT" OF THE ASTRAL PLANE.

BACK INTO YOUR BODY...

WITH A BUMP! BUT WITHOUT LEARNING ANYTHING NEW...

BUT IF YOU JUST HANG ON, WHEN EVERYTHING HAS CALMED DOWN A LITTLE, YOU CAN HELP THE BEING COLLECT HIS BEADS OR WHATEVER. KEEP IN MIND THAT HE HAS HAD TO WORK JUST AS HARD AS YOU TO LEARN HOW TO HOLD ON TO HIS ATTENTION DURING THESE KINDS OF EXPERIENCES.

YOU MAY DISCOVER A JEWEL.

THERE IS NO ESCAPING THE CYCLE OF CONTRACTION AND EXPANSION, AS IT IS A BASIC PRINCIPLE OF LIFE, ON EARTH AS IT IS IN THE ASTRAL PLANE.

YOUR MUSCLES EXPAND AND CONTRACT

YOUR EYES CONTRACT AND EXPAND

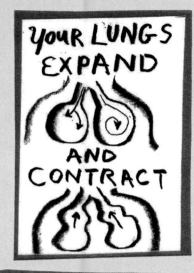

YOUR LUNGS EXPAND AND CONTRACT

BE AWARE OF YOUR STATE. THE "EXPANDED STATE" IS WHEN YOUR CAUSAL BODY CONTRACTS ONLY AFTER REACHING THE POINT OF FULL EXPANSION.

THE "CONTRACTED STATE" IS WHEN YOUR CAUSAL BODY TENDS TO CONTRACT LONG BEFORE REACHING A FULL EXPANSION, OFTEN NEVER EXPANDING FULLY AT ALL, EVER. THIS IS A CHRONIC MISERABLE STATE.

THIS CAN LEAD TO SUDDEN, UNPREDICTABLE, SURPRISE CONTRACTIONS. BESIDES KEEPING YOU ASTRALLY WEAK, IT CAN HAVE DIRE CONSEQUENCES IN YOUR LIFE, LIKE FEARFULNESS, ILLNESS, DEPRESSION AND MORE. SO REMEMBER, PAY ATTENTION TO YOUR ATTENTION!

THIS LAST ONE IS AN ATTENTION-HOLDING EXERCISE. IT WILL HELP YOU TO UNDERSTAND HOW THE ASTRAL AND THE MATERIAL WORLD OVERLAP. BESIDES, IT'S FUN, AND YOU HAVE TO DO IT WITH A FRIEND. HERE'S WHAT YOU NEED.

A CANDLE

A FRIEND

A DARK ROOM

IN THE DARKENED ROOM, SIT NO MORE THAN SEVEN FEET APART, WITH THE CANDLE ON THE FLOOR BETWEEN YOU.

HERE'S THE TRICKY PART. GAZE STEADILY AT YOUR PARTNER, LIKE IN A "STARING CONTEST." DO NOT LOOK INTO THE EYES, DO NOT WATCH THE FACE AT ALL. INSTEAD, CONCENTRATE ALL OF YOUR ATTENTION ON THE SPOT RIGHT IN THE MIDDLE OF THE FOREHEAD, AS IT IS INDICATED IN THIS DRAWING. ⟶

39

NOW, OBSERVE AS THIS FACE "DROPS OUT". OTHER FACES WILL BEGIN TO APPEAR, OLD FACES, YOUNG FACES, ANIMAL FACES...

YOU NEVER KNOW WHAT KINDS OF FACES YOU WILL MEET. OFTEN YOU CAN NOT EVEN TELL WHAT KIND OF FACE IT IS...

IF YOU WANT MORE INFO ON WHAT YOU ARE SEEING, THEN SENSE YOUR FOOT. YOU MAY FIND THIS EXERCISE SHOCKING, AND THAT'S GREAT. A REALLY STRONG TRAVELER IS NEARLY SHOCK-PROOF.

WHAT YOU ARE SEEING IS A KIND OF LIST OF YOUR PARTNER'S OTHER SELVES. BREATHE. THERE IS MUCH TO DISCOVER IN THIS EXERCISE.

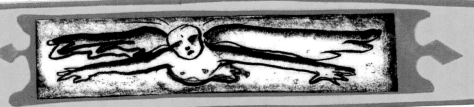

THIS ENDS THE VERY BASICS OF ASTRAL PROJECTION. AS STATED IN THE FOREWORD, THIS ASTRAL PLANE IS A GIFT TO BE DISCOVERED AND EXPLORED BY EACH PERSON LUCKY ENOUGH TO FIND THEIR WAY IN. THERE ARE SO MANY WAYS TO SEE, SO MANY THINGS TO LEARN. WHAT IS PRESENTED HERE IN THIS BOOK IS REALLY JUST A TINY LITTLE PART OF A VAST SUBJECT. A FEW IDEAS, A COUPLE IMPORTANT WORDS, SOME BASIC TOOLS THAT, WHEN YOU DISCOVER HOW TO USE THEM, MORE WILL APPEAR THROUGH A NATURAL PROCESS. THERE IS NO LIMIT TO HOW FAR YOU CAN GO.

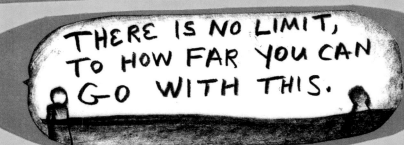

THERE IS NO LIMIT, TO HOW FAR YOU CAN GO WITH THIS.

OUR BODIES ARE ACTUALLY DESIGNED FOR ASTRAL PROJECTION. IT IS OUR BIRTHRIGHT AS HUMAN BEINGS, AND IT IS ALL COMING BACK. THIS TALENT HAS NOT BEEN LOST. IT HAS BEEN, HOWEVER, SADLY FORGOTTEN.

NOW IS THE TIME.

AND WHILE WE ARE REMEMBERING THINGS, LET'S REMEMBER THIS: WE ARE ALL IN THIS WORLD TOGETHER, AND ALL TOGETHER WE FORM A SINGLE BEING OF SUCH AWESOME BEAUTY, POWER AND WISDOM THAT NO SINGLE PERSON COULD EVER EVEN FULLY COMPREHEND IT. SO LET US GET TOGETHER AND BE THIS BEING.

THE TIME IS NOW.

The Author Wishes To Acknowledge:

▷ William BLAKE
▷ EMANUEL Swedenborg
▷ Rudolf Steiner
▷ Dr. ALEJANDRO JUNGER
▷ MAURICE Nicoll
▷ Orly Olofson
▷ ECKHART Tolle
▷ ADI DA SAMRAJ
▷ MARINA GUINNESS
▷ WILHELM REICH
▷ PATANJALI
▷ DRUNVALO MELCHIZEDEK
▷ MOM AND DAD   THANKS
                GUYS.

ALSO BY BRASS TACKS PRESS

Available at <u>www.brasstackspress.com</u>

Thirty Days on Spring

Richard McDowell

Stories about Spring Street by a Downtown LA Poet Laureate.

Topanga Beach Snake Pit: Vol. 1

Baretta

Topanga Beach stories from the '70s and '80s.

Topanga Beach Experience

Paul Lovas
Pablo Capra

Topanga Beach stories from the '60s and '70s.

The Mystery Man from The Magic Band

Herb Bermann

Captain Beefheart's writing partner revealed.

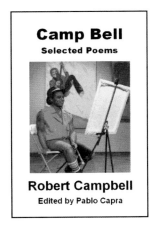

Camp Bell: Selected Poems

Robert Campbell

"You can hear it on a moonlit night when the wind chants..."

Eight Years

Paul Roessler

Musician for Nina Hagen and The Screamers muses in poetry.

FIRST!

Pablo Capra, ed.

Comments from the early days of YouTube.

Little Nuts

Alden Marin

How short can a poem be? Or are you just being a little nuts?

Made in the USA
Columbia, SC
21 June 2021